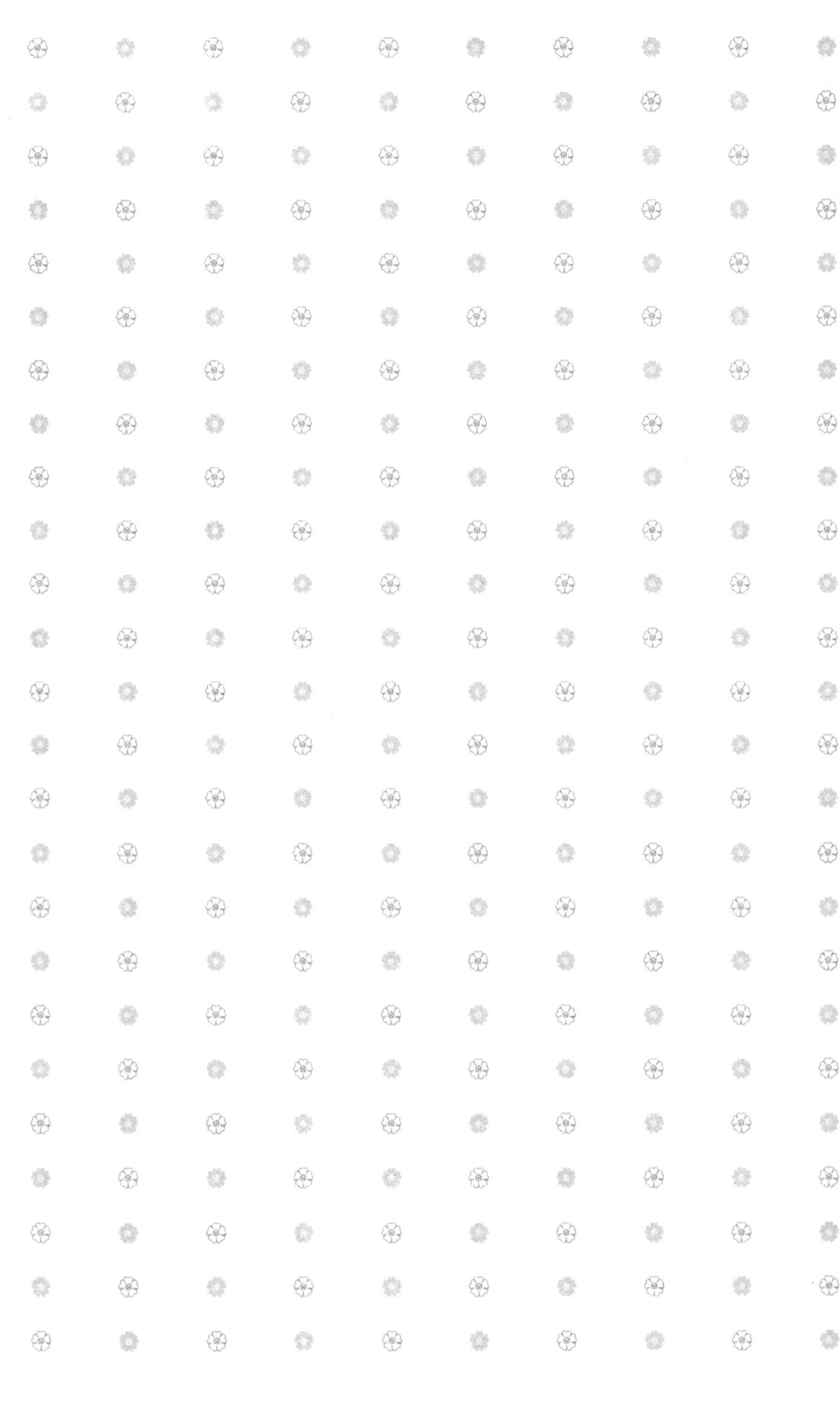

in case of emergency press

We are proud to acknowledge the Traditional Owners of country throughout Australia and to recognise their continuing connection to land, waters, and culture. We pay our respects to their Elders.

We support recognition, reconciliation, and reparation.

Ditching the Guff

Veronica Cookson

in case of emergency press
https://icoe.com.au
Travancore, Victoria
Australia

Published by in case of emergency press Keywords

Copyright © Veronica Cookson Keywords
All rights reserved. Without limiting the rights under copyright reserved above, no part of this publication may be reproduced, stored in or introduced into a database and retrieval system or transmitted in any form or any means (electronic, mechanical, photocopying, recording or otherwise) without the prior written permission of both the owner of copyright and the above publishers.

ISBN: 978-1-7637749-3-3

Cover design: Ward Nikriph

Acknowledgements

Some of these poems appear in *New Poets 'Legacy'* 2021.

Positive Words from February 2014, October 2014, December 2014, December 2016, August 2017, September 2017, October 2017, January 2018, February 2018.

Mozzie 2018, May 2019, June 2019, October 2020, March 2021, August 2021, August 2022, October 2022.

Friendly Street Anthologies, 2006, 2007, 2013, 2014, 2015, (Poem of the Month 2017), 2018, 2020, 2023.

Valley Micro Press (New Zealand) June 2018.
Victor Harbor Times September 2023.

Milang Community News, Poet's Corner, March 2021 and March 2023

Thanks to Lindy Warrell, Louise Nicholas and Helen Hutton.

On-going thanks to Ochre Coast Poets for regular critiquing.

For David, my husband and best friend.
Also, for my family, always supportive.

Table of Contents

Threadbare 1
    Happy Families 3
    The Old Place 4
    The Nature of Nurturing 6
    Renmark Re-run 7
    Genes 8
    Swaps 9
    Twelve Suits 10
    Snake 12
    Poem for Christine 13
    Pinching Peaches 14
    Secrets 15
    A Beautiful Game 16
    A Case in Point 18
    Rusty Wheels 19
    Making a Meal of it 20
    Teacher 21
    Keeping it Uniform 22
    A Reckoning 23
Changing Times 25
    Factory Ladies 27
    Girls Day In 28
    Eighteen 29
    Bad Boys 30
    Welsh Love Spoon 31
    All The Years 32
    Pulped Fiction 33
    Low Flying 34
    Outback Highway 35
    Heatwave 36
    Scotch Mist 37
    Puddles 38

 Beach Invasion 39
 Patsy Patchwork 40
 Gimme Chocolate 41
 Penong Races 42
 Egg-sposé 43
 On The Side 44
 Traffic Lights 45

Adoption Adaption 47
 Runaway 49
 Unit Seven 50
 Change 51
 Shopping List... 52
 Dinner Dance 54
 Through the Wall 55
 In the Interim 56
 Safeguards 57
 Once More 58
 A Most Unlikely Love Letter 59
 Glenda 60
 Autumn Morning 61
 By Her Own Hand 62
 Could Have Been My Story 64
 Grease Monkeys 65
 Legacy 66
 A set of Wheels 67
 Yesterdays and Tomorrow 68
 Sculpting Poems 69
 Matriarch 70
 Caffeine Fix 71
 Still Learning 72
 Safe Bet 73
 Number 24 74
 Adoption Adaption 75

About the Author 77

Ditching the Guff

Veronica Cookson

Even the darkest night will end
and the sun will rise.

Victor Hugo—Les Misérables

Threadbare

Threadbare, ravaged by love—
as who amongst us is not.

Karen Joy Fowler

Happy Families

Baby Boomer days meant fewer cars when
rowdy groups of kids shared the freedom
of street games with busted bikes and billycarts,
skippy, hopscotch and knucklebones.
When we played dress-ups, we pretended
to be royals in ragged robes: no drunken fights,
empty bellies, or over-burdened mums.

In our half of a Housing Trust double unit
with a dividing wall that leaked secrets,
we took no notice of an odd neighbour
with pink elephant hallucinations,
or another who chopped up furniture.
We avoided one with DTs
and scaly lizard skin while all around,
children shook empty money boxes when other
desperate fingers had plundered them.

One wife came with her bottle-ravaged man
to beg my dipso dad help him find work—
hoping this time, overworked promises
might be more than blown glass.
And when all the fathers died early
from battles where, like *Groundhog Day*,
each dawn was as hopeless as the last,
mothers glued their families back together.

The Old Place

For Mum, in appreciation

They were the happiest years of her marriage,
she would say later, spent in a humble hut
in scrub outside town at Proper Bay;
dirt floors, no electricity or running water.

Those happiest years meant
three children born before she knew it,
rain-water's slow trickle into a tank,
doled out mean as a miser from dishes to floors,
the maximum squeezed from each drop,
frozen chunks of rainbow for the ice chest,
delivered with tongs, finding one last sliver
in the meltdown, ambrosia, savoured slowly
on fiery furnace nights.

Those happiest years meant
a washing machine worked by hand
and even nappies pressed with 'Mrs Potts'
flat irons, heated year-round on the green
and cream Metters No 1, red child-sized
kero lamps with full-sized acrid smell,
nights with moving, looming shadows
hiding monsters, but only just.

Ditching the Guff

Those happiest years meant
watered down milk, cream skimmed before
delivery by Nick, their old Greek neighbour,
hunting rabbits to augment meals, skins
turned furry sides in, hand stitched into slippers
for tiny feet and a husband returning home
in the ancient buck-board.

Those happiest years of her marriage really meant
before they moved into town
and he started going to the pub.

The Nature of Nurturing

There's rivalry in a home with many children.
Each day, I snuck into the kitchen in pyjamas
when Mum began her early morning routine.

I watched her scrape ashes
from the grate before building a fire—
scrunching newspaper, adding wood chips,
carefully feeding the timid sparks till they flared.
Then she'd take Dad's cuppa in bed, a priority.
Next, the saucepan of Blue Lake Flaked Oats,
quietly soaked at the back of the stove overnight,
on the hob for breakfast.

I don't recall what Mum and I spoke about—
likely I prattled of childish trifles.
My siblings unaware that I'd grabbed
this one-to-one time, closely guarding
it as a secret, never once considering
that a mother may need time
to herself.

Renmark Re-run

Car trips for May holidays held certainties; being part of a four-kid squabble in the back seat, anticipating scoffing huge oranges for five shillings a wheat bag. Vats at Berri were Dad's cue for a theatrical sniff of air redolent with fermenting grapes as we all joked how long it would take him to drink the lot.

At the park, siblings reclaimed a wonder-land of willows rooted in a dense mat of debris, reaching out into the river. We only had to walk across, under those weeping fronds, to be out of sight on a virtual island, so enticing, we'd leave only for meals or bed. Dad fished at his favourite spot, in his hand-knitted fawn cardi, waiting for Murray cod to bite.

Today, courtesy of powered pruners, grapevines have had their yearly hair-cut, like knobbly heads of upended yard brooms, bristles Mohawk'd to a uniform length and we buy our oranges encased in red-mesh, without any oversized rejects from the Co-op.

The caravan park is still there; the willows as well, though the river's reclaimed our secret playground. There are boxy cabins now, strewn like junk where Dad fished in his hand-knitted fawn cardi. If there'd been the new Murray cod regulations, he likely would have high-tailed it across the river to the Paringa pub, spent his days there instead.

Genes

As a child, I thought my Nanna unique,
eccentric to some, exotic as the parrots she kept,
an Aladdin's Cave of knickknacks jumbled on walls,
always treats of baked biscuits, lollies from a jar.

From the dark haired, clear skinned bias
of endless youth, came teenage judgement.
Saw Grandmother's slow shuffle, soft slippers
worn year round, their heels crushed inwards.
Vowed I wouldn't do that.

Heard Grandmother with her sisters
share the world's biggest joke,
like farm house chooks, all a-cackle together.
Swore I wouldn't sound like that.

Caught just a glimpse of brown eyes
that crinkled at the slightest excuse
almost vanished into a street map of laugh lines.
Didn't want my skin to end up like that.

Saw Grandmother, Aunties, a roly-poly army,
crimson, orange, purple patterned pinnies
covering lumpy breasts, non-existent waists.
Promised myself that wouldn't be me.

I can imagine my Nanna,
that fountainhead of our gene pool
and know she's had the last laugh.

Swaps

For Vicki

Our parents did their best,
Christmas, two pint-sized daughters
barely enough money to go round.
One girl would get a pram
the other, a doll
but that festive morning
as I discovered my stroller
spied Vicki's toy.

Saw Shirley Temple's golden curls
cobalt eyes that blinked open and shut
dimpled smile in creamy china cheeks
wearing a summer dress, with undies,
glanced again at *my* gift, decision made.
With a four-year-old's guile
showed off the buggy's charms to my sibling
its pastel pink and blue painted body
shiny wheels coloured to match, pressed
the handle so she could hear it cry *Mama*.

Our parents were nonplussed, but it was easy
a two-year-old sister wasn't in the hunt.
The doll was mine—
I called her Elizabeth.

Twelve Suits

Our family had not seen this sight before;
a dozen men in wrinkled suits moved quietly past.
Fresh-faced youths and seasoned hands
with beards overfilled our lounge room with navy
and brown bulk, plus an overt male stink of whisky
and stale tobacco.
My father had been a merchant seaman—when he
missed that life, drifted to the wharf to connect
with men on any British ship in port, normally
bringing one or two home, unannounced,
for their first taste of a good old Aussie welcome.
He'd outdone himself this time.

Though my mother had already provided a meal
for six kids, courtesy demanded she feed
these extras, gob-smacked at this turn of events.
Burr and brogue were alien; we struggled
to understand as they reminisced, eagerly pulling
family photos from wallets.
Reluctantly, I allowed myself to be coaxed
to the piano; but so nervous, it was a poor show,
hardly worth their excessive praise.
Rowdy voices over-rode one another,
calling for more, naming requests.

Ditching the Guff

Next day some men came back with ornaments,
souvenirs from Middle Eastern and Asian ports
but when Dad confessed a need for blankets,
these were spirited off ship onto beds, an action
tantamount to theft by these men, but willingly
carried out as a thank-you for our hospitality.

Under my warm covers, I dreamt of those sailors;
wondered if the whole ship's crew
had been invited and we were lucky
only twelve showed up.

Snake

Mum was a crack shot
old rifle always close by, ready
to pot rabbits or predators.
Danger didn't register when we kids
played outside, seemed almost a game
when she checked our scrub yard
beforehand.

There was fear in her voice one day
when she ordered us inside—
a snake, sunning itself outside the door;
enough for Mum to grab the gun.
My siblings were tiptoe on a kero box
fingers straining at the window-sill,
anxious, peering out to watch Mum
hurriedly sight up
see her shoulder drop with a sudden jolt
hear the loud 'bang'.

Later the snake would join its kin
as a deadly brown streamer
slung over our green painted gate.
My Father's voice echoes across the years:
Just as well your Mother's a good shot—
that's three of the buggers this week.

It wouldn't do today—
laws and conservation stuff
and maybe I'd try to shoo the snake away
if my kids strayed too close.
Maybe.

Poem for Christine

I don't know why she called me 'Princess'.
An ungainly girl with a tiresome giggle,
ginger hair, freckles to match,
dowdy dresses one size too big.

Christine shared her family's whacko faith.
When she brought her Bible to school,
remained blind and deaf to other kids' mockery.
Though sympathetic, I wanted no-one
to mistake us for mates
and cringed as she tried to stroke my hair
as though I was a doll to be fondled.
Fleeing that fawning attention didn't work—
Christine just followed me like Mary's little lamb.

My best friend moving away was the catalyst
for months of misery from bullying threats,
cold shoulders, vandalized workbooks.
Only one girl talked to me then;
she called me 'Princess'.

Pinching Peaches

At home in the 50s, Dad dished out discipline;
his strap, hung behind our kitchen door,
a warning against children's cheek.
As a dictator wields tariffs to have his way,
the leer of the strap enough.

Mum, a stay-at-home housewife;
time filled with the tedium of every day.
Her garden boasted vegies and two fruit trees.
Apricots morphed into jam fit for Gods,
preserves served with custard for many desserts.

Our peaches had skin any female would envy;
plump, glowing with promise; a rosy hue more natural
than Revlon rouge; flesh, luscious with juice,
as only a home-grown could be.
But, Dad's tree—kids forbidden.

When peaches were a tick from ripening,
pickpocket slick, we siblings snaffled a few.
Salivating over the feast to come,
we pedalled our bone-shakers
to cubbies in nearby ti-tree scrub.

Ambrosia ran down our chins as we slurped
our spoils in secret, sucked fingers
sticky as molasses—shared grins
wrought revenge over Dad's power
and Mum's submission.

Secrets

My father, a silver-tongued raconteur,
took his children on magic carpet rides with tales
of mischief from Vladivostok to Valparaiso.
A likely lad who ran away to sea aged fourteen,
jumped ship at 31, met and beguiled my mother.

At eighteen, she was a '10'.
When Dad saw her thighs, belly, breasts
descend stairs towards him, he gawped,
lusted like a voyeur at a peep show.
He vowed on the spot they'd marry,
have six kids. She laughed, called him crazy,
yet eight weeks later tied the knot.

No hint of a worm in the apple—
Dad forgot to say he'd changed his name,
he had abandoned a wife,
two sons and a daughter
on the other side of the world.

When I think of my father's deceit,
both households unaware, I wonder
how that other family coped, expecting
his homecoming with more stories
of derring-do from foreign ports.
Waiting, waiting.
Endlessly hoping.

A Beautiful Game

Dad was a soccer fan; for him,
the game's focus on fancy foot work,
no hand passes, beat Aussie Rules
every which way.
Keen, he offered our family's services
when a call went out
to take over the league canteen.

So, every Sunday we set up shop
behind a window in the club rooms,
with popular confectionery and chips
tempting us constantly in colourful cartons
stored Monday to Saturday at home.

Country sport in the late 50s
began with Marching Girls;
short skirts swinging, tall caps, chin straps,
red jackets, gold braid epaulets,
white gloves and calf-length boots,
Coppertone legs flashing up down up down,
keeping time to Stars and Stripes Forever
and Colonel Bogie.

Dad mooched with mates while we cheered
aging Italians, Greeks, Yugoslavs and Dutch
practising headers before the game—
bandy legs with knobbly knees
that escaped over-long shorts,
high socks almost masking shin-guards
and liniment.

Ditching the Guff

We siblings had a powerful incentive
to help Mum when she vowed to quit—
thoughts of chocolate
we could quietly snaffle later,
from under eagle eyes of parents
who never counted their stock.

A Case in Point

When I was 11, in grade six, my parents couldn't
pay to replace my broken school case. Friends
gave them a bar-fridge-sized suitcase to use
as my school work hold-all. It was that, or nothing.
At the school bus-stop, amongst rows of kitbags,
boys' leather school bags and girls' cases, mine
was a giant's belly, wherein a few exercise books,
pencils, packed lunch and plastic cordial bottle
rattled around.

When my best friend changed schools that year,
other students bullied me—gave me cold shoulders,
vandalised books, destroyed my lunch. They already
laughed out loud, pointing to that old cardboard
Globite. One afternoon riding home on the bus,
three girls not in my class sat across the aisle
at the front, heads together, whispering, their
malicious eyes flicking back, faces intent.

When they jumped out at my stop, I stayed shivering
in my seat, while they stood in wait, before
re-boarding. As I got off a block away, they followed
then fenced me in, closer, closer. I grabbed
that loathed bit of luggage, whirled it around
like a wrecking ball, again and again. The girls
slunk away. I walked home shaken but untouched,
adrenaline pumping and although that tote
was an indignity, sometimes bigger is better.

Rusty Wheels

At 12, for Christmas I scored
a brand new BSA bike—26 inches
of black and chrome with deadly
brake grips on the handle bars.
On HP, ill afforded, it had the caveat
that each day I lug it out of the weather
up five steep cement steps.

I always forgot this promise,
much like an MP's pledge,
till drumbeats on the roof
told me I needed to rescue
my metal steed, tackle a hurried
bump bump bumping up
to the shelter of the back verandah.

As sure as shame, my once-prized
two-wheeler corroded, arousing remorse
over years. Even now, there's a shred
of concern when storms threaten,
remembering that unkept vow,
wondering if, in my laxity, I'd left
anything of value out in the rain.

Guilt, the colour of neglect.

Making a Meal of it

As a child, I was shocked to see my mother crying with Dad's two week's wages in hand, from his job, swapped from working full-time in the cold stores, to smallgoods at our local abattoir, dubbed 'The Freezers' by locals, plus part-time bar tending. Priority one, rent. Next, Dad's regular allowance, then with all our household goods, from car through to Mixmaster paid off, with interest, to a hire purchase mob, her despair grew, realising that no matter how she shuffled the figures, she could not find cash for food.

Once Dad began working with offal, in desperation, Mum was forced to accept his pilfering of animal offcuts deemed of little value. Yet this bounty formed phobias: a life-long gagging reflex thinking about the grey murk of brains, or lookalike sweetbreads, plus vomit-inducing tripe. Then there was peeling sandpaper skin from cooked ox-tongues before they vanished into a pottery bowl, covered with a saucer, weighed down to become brawn. Nicer, were meals of bread, fried in suet—fatty, filling. We grilled sliced beef hearts, tender, tasty as T-bones, on the top of the wood stove.

At a friend's house, her family helped themselves to pineapple quinces or apples, crisp as an Autumn morning, stored in a sturdy box in the kitchen. With their blessing, I enjoyed them too. Apples at our home were doled out sparingly, a once-a-week treat, that would have been on level pegging with lollipops, were we ever to be offered those.

I will never forget my mother's endless struggle to pay bills and feed us as best she could in the face of crushing odds. Even more profound though, her tears on Dad's pay day.

Teacher

College fresh, barely older than her pupils
she was timid as a wild bird,
hems modestly lower than average,
necklines defensively higher.

A hen bird's drab, she blended
into the classroom's dun—
a bun of sparrow-brown hair
drum-skin tight low on her neck,
nose, a neat beak between watchful eyes.
Blood pressure on each cheek, king parrot's red.

Students knew they had the upper hand
as she moved around the room on avian legs.
With elbows pinioned to each side, biro in hand,
she extended a forearm, pointing to each child
in turn, her chirp struggling to carry.

Did this teacher breathe easier at each
lesson's end, her emotional relief echoing
like wind sighing through the classroom?
Did her charges feel it too?

I got an 'A' for English under the teacher's wing.
An eagle, after all.

Keeping it Uniform

In high school, I wanted to stay home when
we were too poor to replace filled exercise books.
So, cramped cursive quickly clogged just the one—
each subject marked by telltale dog-eared pages.
Wanted to bolt after borrowing typing paper
from kind friends, who had no expectations.

Though siblings' shoes had sieve-like soles
sopping up rain, inserts cut from Weetbix packets
kept their toes hidden. Mine were clearly visible
in outgrown lace-ups with upper and underside
edges split apart, gaping like gossipers' mouths.
I tried to hide my feet under the desk.
Everyone knew. No-one commented.

In shapeless hand-me-downs, my sister and I stood out
from mates in their navy permanent-press box pleats.
At thirteen, blouses were tight, too tight—
sleeves too short for July's icy squalls, too long
for February's fire. A threadbare blazer
hiding my arms, shouted the reality.
Uniforms aren't what they're meant to be.

A Reckoning

After a life of heavy drinking and smoking,
Dad had a stroke at fifty-three. Enfeebled
by repeated episodes, he became a baby
battling Goliath, a foe that bashed
him backwards in a ruthless race to regression.
The geriatric ward became his home.

We children seldom visited the pyjama'd,
medicated men flopped in chairs
like store dummies outside their rooms,
Dad's face, just one blank among the many,
his useless hand cupped in the good—cheap,
dark-framed glasses askew. He always cried
at the sight of us, whether for himself, his family,
or for life's unfairness, we never knew.

Then pneumonia struck. Against the rules
a kindly nurse told Mum, on doctor's orders,
there was nothing they could do. Shocked,
she railed against the sentence
but medical science was law;

left behind, the memory of Dad's larrikin voice,
the bawdy jokes and Mum's joyful laugh
as he waltzed her around the kitchen.

Changing Times

As the present now will later be past,
for the times they are a-changin'...

— *Bob Dylan*

Factory Ladies

A song by Donna Summer shrieks
against the thump, thump of twin graders,
vibrating metal monsters, fit to deafen.
As in prison, old hands show us what to do—
we bow our heads like supplicants,
concentrate on beheading prawns,
thumbs dig in, pull apart, faster, faster.

Boredom is a killer so it's distracting
when a woman farts, a putrid pong,
ignores her fellows as they swear, move away,
works on alone in a fusty garlic cloud—knows
whatever anyone says, hard cash doesn't stink.
Sex talk soaks the tea breaks—
who wants it, who gets it and how;
lurid ins and outs more than anyone needs to know.

This windowless, corrugated box is the world
but at 4.30, screeching music still in our ears,
we are free to race home on aching legs,
minds numb to begin home chores anew.
We'll be back again tomorrow, on the line,
with iceberg water, stabs from vengeful prawns,
and Donna Summer's vocals pounding a mantra
bosses hope will spur and inspire.

Yes, we work hard for the money.

Girls Day In

An ideal arrangement—
husbands at work, kids at school.
Three of us alternated homes, meeting
now and then when we had no work.
One supplied a cask, the others,
party pies, potato chips, Tim Tams.
All day long, we laughed like lunatics,
played records, nibbled, drank.

There's just the haziest memory of once
when my elder daughter was off school, sick.
Instead of changing our plans,
she came with me to meet my friends, later
reporting as time went on, we grew rowdier,
the jokes raunchier, gossip crazier,
complaints about bosses, bitchier. Then,
while we tunelessly sang along to ELO,
The Cars and *Supertramp*, it seems that
I suggested we could form our own pop group,
call ourselves *The Moselles*.

I can't help but wonder at the madness
of driving home after all that booze
and just what I would have suggested
for our band's name had we been swigging
shots of plum Slivovitz or cherry Wiśniówka.

Eighteen

For Denis

His name leaps from the death notices
a friend's first boyfriend.
The briefest summary of a life
constrained by price per line.
Strangers claim him as partner, patriarch,
clearly, he'd moved away from the reach of rumour
then: 'died suddenly, aged 72'.

I try to imagine him that old
but the snapshot in my memory is eighteen
dark hair combed to a neat duck's bum
his EK Holden, sunshine yellow and white,
lashings of chrome proudly polished like a prize.

No way to know how life had shaped him.
Each time I open my mental album of photos
he'll be here, unblemished by baldness or beer gut,
eighteen—forever
driving off into the sunset in that Holden.

Bad Boys

He strides to water's edge, eager for waves
seventy plus, but tanned body muscular
confident, indifferent to opinion
budgie almost strangled in black racing bathers
bad boy emblazoned in white across his bum
with each step its cartoon eyes wink suggestively
that downward slash of mouth
becomes a leer.

He crosses paths with a teenager
bare chest pale, fragile as eggshells
wearing the uniform of his peers;
knee-length shorts, sodden,
prickly as wet wool
dragging and chafing pubes.

Youth dismisses age with barely a glance—
he reckons the baddest thing
about any old codger
has to be that logo.

Welsh Love Spoon

'In Passing' by Brian Harris

To be born in Wales, not with silver spoon
in your mouth but with music
in your blood and with poetry
in your soul is a privilege indeed.

My cousin's fingers traced the spoon
her sweetheart poured his soul into
hand-carved from a piece of Welsh oak,
decorated with Celtic symbols,
wood-grained hearts, chains, padlock—
pledging love, faithfulness, security;
a twisted stem confirming his hope
they would always be entwined likewise.

No everyday wooden spoon this,
with furred edges from over-use
made to stir oatmeal or lamb cawl,
but a love spoon, to be cherished.
Sealed, polished with natural beeswax,
shiny as her mother's silver tablespoon,
it will hold pride of place in their kitchen
outlasting rusty racks of trophy teaspoons.

She will give him the answer he yearns
imagining cold nights together in bed—
spooning.

All The Years

They sit together, distant—
her lips a lemon twist
his nose an eagle's beak.
Girls nuzzled that honker, ran fingers
through hair grown scraggy
as sea-wrack after ebb tides.
And *her* hair—how she purred
as he massaged her scalp
then combed the silken mane.
How did it become steel wool
tamed only by brush and spray?

The voice he loved to hear sing for joy
developed more than a pinch of petulance
as he, bronzed demigod,
watched his tan turn to age freckles
enough to join the dots.
Her body, a voluptuous young Loren
envied, lusted over
slumped, tubby as a Toby jug.
Their firm skin now wrinkled as walnuts;
eyes once bright with love grown dim.

They sit together, distant—
till he leans over, gently whispers
then enfolds her hands in his.

Pulped Fiction

For Brian

He plans to break the book through its spine
after Chapter 41, when Johnny proposes to Stella,
take only the unread portion on his holiday.
This second-hand sex romp,
tawdry as a faded courtesan
has plots cheesecloth flimsy.
Almost a kilo of titillation
too heavy to add to his luggage,
is more than likely to self-combust.

It tickles him that on this trip, he will shed,
chapter by chapter, 194 pages into waste-paper
baskets across the globe.
Maybe Chapter 42, with Emma & Rob's
steamy sex will stay behind in Auckland
and the part when Stella & Johnny break up,
remains in La Paz.
24 pages later, as Tom realizes he loves Stella,
his tour will reach South Georgia.
In Terra Del Fuego, he'll leave behind the bit
where Cassandra's world falls apart.

After Rebecca tries in vain to kill Emma,
it's Chapter 69. Goodness prevails—
they all live happily-ever-after.
He'll ditch that last piece of guff
from an icebreaker off Antarctica.

Low Flying

Christopher Reeve, aka Superman,
spent his last years confined
to a wheelchair, fighting for life.
Brought down, not by kryptonite,
but a fall from a horse.
Man of Steel consigned to celluloid.

That alter-ego came to mind
when I saw an old man cross the street,
his Gopher, red as summer berries
with a cobalt cloth
fastened rakishly to the head-rest,
draped like a curtain at his back.

As he took off down the footpath,
a breeze played with the fabric,
teased and lifted the folds
till they fluttered cape-like behind him.
I could almost see that gold and blood-red logo.

At least in this century, he is not on crutches,
or battling to leave a cane bathchair.
He makes his own rules—and flies.

Outback Highway

We open car windows,
hypnotised by the thrum-thrum of tyres
on this endless stretch of blacktop.

Away from roadsides,
parched desert dwellers,
mulga struggles among saltbush,
while spinifex holds on
prickly as spiteful lovers.

No traffic to grab attention,
except for the odd shimmering mirage.
Only the bitumen littered with highway gore
proves that others were here before us.
Raptors lift from road-kill.
Once we've disappeared they'll binge again.

Signs of humanity proclaim 'Drowsy drivers die'
against a washed-out water-colour sky.
150 kilometres from Camooweal.

Heatwave

When bad light stops play at beach cricket
and dogs are too tired to chase balls,
after sandcastles are flattened
and children's squeals go silent,
a bonfire sun sizzles into the sea
and technicolour shelters are packed away.

Once the car-park empties
of salt-pickled bodies and boogie boards,
the beach is ours, to pick up plastic bags,
broken yellow spades, empty Coke cans,
dead fireworks and doggy poo packages,
discarded like yesterday's promises.
We relish the quiet, brief rulers of our realm.

Tomorrow's another scorcher.
They'll be back.

Scotch Mist

Barely there dampness
seeps over everything
chokes out joy
a spectral grey cloud
too puny to form drops
to splatter, colourless petals
on dull cement.

Hopeless haze
is hardly heavy enough
to dewdrop hair
and this insipid miasma
is a blotting paper
that soaks up noise
dials our world mute.

Street-lights' pallid glow
just a ghost image of sun.
As day surrenders to night,
pong of wood smoke
taints the pewter sky.

Not enough though
for the rain gauge.

Puddles

Walking in light rain, I pick my way
around latte-coloured puddles,
their surfaces speckled with steady driblets,
as rain sprinkles my face.

My mind back-pedals to childhood,
crouching to peer at my reflection,
to the thrill of jumping into mud pools,
over and over, feeling the mucky wetness
splash up my legs, turning skirt and knickers
into sodden scraps—knowing I'd be in trouble
for that—and waterlogged shoes.
Better still, I discarded boots and socks,
to jump in barefooted, frog-like,
delighting in the squish.

Now, I fight the urge
to peel off sandals, experience the squelch,
like squashed slugs between my pinkies
yet again.

Beach Invasion

At sun's early suggestion, families
pattern their patch with beach towels
strike shelters every which way into sand
slop sun-screen over winter-white bodies
lick spring's first ice-creams from the kiosk
bring with them a salt and vinegar whiff
of childhood's hot chips in newspaper.

Cars 'doof-doof' along the esplanade,
vie with squeals of children
immune to water's chill
as they chase each other in the shallows.
Till a cold breeze heralds the westerly:
winter's last cloud foils the sun—
brollies folded away with a castanet snap
sand shrugged from towels.

In a flash, the strangers are gone.
Seaweed strewn like mouldy straw
a pink Barbie sandal
left behind.

Patsy Patchwork

Uninvited, she stayed.
Scraps of tortoiseshell and terracotta
patched her white fur like daubs of paint,
a whisker away from ugly.

Smelling the roses came naturally—
taking ballerina steps through flower beds,
pausing, snuffling stamens
to emerge smiling, cartoon-like,
with a pollen-budding button nose.

Months later, floral arrangements
for a daughter's wedding
adorned our coffee table.
Amid the merrymaking, we found Patsy.
No welcoming miaow. She was stiff. Dead.

Next day, dusting around the blooms,
my hands froze at the sight
of ghostly paw prints
in the dust on glass,
too soon to wipe them away.

Gimme Chocolate

My habit is inherited—
you could expect little else when father
pandered to mother's pregnancy cravings
with a block of Caramello every day
for seven months, at least.

There are those who don't like chocolate.
Not for them, the delicious quandary
whether to suck slowly or scoff
Peppermint Crisp or Flake, Mars Bar or Snickers.
Nor for them, a shape of comfortable curves
from too many Polly Waffles and Curly Wurlys.

But for an addict with caramel in her veins
anything less than total indulgence is tough
and I know about the perils of withdrawal.
So, till I find the strength to face my demons,
I take comfort in a jumbo packet of Smarties.

Penong Races

This once-a-year social event at Nullarbor's edge
draws a mob from near and far, excitable
as Melbourne Cup devotees.

Ladies proud as city cousins
in chiffon and lace split thigh-high,
fascinators and hats in colours of the rainbow
rub shoulders with workmen's stubbies and thongs.
Younger sisters totter in oversized stilettos,
tug awkwardly at their borrowed strapless frocks.
Boys in suits, ties, baseball caps sideways,
all flashy as cockerels.

Steak sandwiches, hot dogs,
home-made cake replenished like Magic Puddings
delayed by a rush to the fence for each race
with cheers or curses at the finishing post.
Then, on to the make-shift bar, a plank perched
across two 44-gallon drums.

Cash prizes draw young fillies and older mares
for 'Fashion on Field' under a brutal blue sky.
They parade across dry dusty grass, winners equal
to Derby Day. A pungent zephyr of mothballs
drifts above the lot and a country news
photographer snaps for his social pages.

Egg-sposé

They perch together at our fortnightly market,
hard boiled, no use for fancies.
She, glasses over gimlet eyes in ovoid face,
sells eggs, scruffy sweetcorn and other stuff,
cash box close by for change, while he,
in a cap of white feathers,
scabby legs poking from shorts,
scatters wisecracks like seed.

Both cackle a warning they might cheat us
and we believe just that; if we let them.
The pair scratch out enough black money
from a small holding to stretch their pension,
growing seasonal vegies, raising chooks,
trading at multiple markets.
Not above sneaking in a broken egg
or others with shitty streaks.

Two ageing chickens—
an Australorp hen's dark plumes,
a battle-scarred White Leghorn rooster;
it seems this diverse duo
pecks along just fine.

On The Side

She knows the sound of his car,
holds her breath till she hears
the signal; a beep, then a gear change
when the XP drives around the corner.
She waits by the side gate.

Kids are asleep; she can't go out
but he can visit for a time, hold her close,
make her smile, snatch a little happiness
however brief, from the bleak.
Comfort more than grand passion
they are no Taylor and Burton—
she wonders if neighbours know.

Little more than a child herself
no telephone, can't drive.
Her husband works all hours.
When home, brutal words, gaslighting,
keeps visitors away with rudeness.
Yet, when life is at its loneliest, her lover
appears as if he hears her silent call.

This thread between two people
with other lives, is more powerful
than the fear of being caught.

Traffic Lights

In a couple's dating days,
on best behaviour, she's just cruising,
green lights all the way.
An odd speed hump is short-term amber,
before remorse, reassurances
and makeup sex steers her back to green.

But driving conditions often quickly change.
When a wife finds she is always at fault,
she negotiates eggshells in her amber world,
unwittingly provoking the red stop sign;
attempting to navigate blind corners, road works,
sudden speed shifts. Amber Red Amber Red.

More colours could be added to the range.
Indigo, to signal *danger danger*—
off the expressway, unsure which lane
to merge into from roundabouts,
on guard for unexpected traffic
ready to cut a partner off.

But purple is most effective.
When slowing for chicanes, almost
run off the road by a steamrolling tailgater,
green lights fade into memory.
Once identity's lost, give-way is all one-way,
purple would flash, go—*now*.

What she'd really like is to just freewheel.

Adoption Adaption

Things change. Stuff happens.
Life goes on.

Elizabeth Scott

Runaway

Then he had that .22. Always loaded, it menaced from a corner, until an exchange became so heated, we physically fought for the gun but with his extra strength, I feared the end. As soon as he left for work, I hid two packed suitcases of clothing, shoes, and precious photos. Then, with a handbag full of personal effects, I fled my small country town, to Adelaide to meet a mate. I trembled like a felon before the rope as my mother drove me to the airport. Later she said she waited to watch the plane leave, knowing once away, I would be out of danger.

My friend took me to my temporary refuge, her home in the hills. Too stressed to calm down, drinking too many coffees, my panic flooded the kitchen. The phone ringing rattled us both. I heard the voice ask if I was there, listened to her put him off my trail. As a teacher, after a day's classroom stress, she craved relaxation, peace; no angst. Equally, I needed to talk—a therapist may have been a better option.

Often, I took a bus into the city. Strange streets slowly became familiar. Social Security allocated benefits. Warned of his threat of steel capped boots and locked room, they kept my whereabouts hidden at espionage level.
I became a silent voter.

Sometimes I walked to Mount Barker to buy food for our shared dinner. Soon, my former protector made it clear she wanted her space with its sacred silence to herself again. My new life had to begin. With part-time work at a city shop, I could almost afford a tiny unit on the CBD edge.

Unit Seven

Back then, the price of freedom,
paying hard-earned rent
for a poky first floor joint in a tower block
op-shops scoured for table, bed, two chairs
small change scraped up for soup
to last the week, footsteps of noisy neighbours
echoing in dark stairwells.

Back then, the price of freedom,
a constant glance over shoulders, hasty scan
of cars at kerbs before setting out.
Always near the door in coffee shops,
then scuttle back, a frightened mouse,
to the bolt hole of Unit Seven with
nightmares of forced return to previous life.

Back then, the price of freedom,
a tear-laden physical wrench
away from family and friends.
To stand alone, drink in hand,
at a window in pitch-black room,
to watch red, gold city lights
wink away, indifferent—
with a backdrop of radio voices
a paltry echo of human contact.

To look back now is to marvel at the journey,
a panic filled roller coaster ride,
through blind corners with sudden
nose-dives—eyes wide open.

To start again was the only choice.

Change

My home town has moved on.
Gone, the jeweller's with its stoop
dark as Old Gold chocolate;
the furnishers boasting
they stood behind every bed they sold.
On the corner. handicrafts hang within
once-sacred walls where Sunday Psalms
no longer soar past stained-glass saints.

The electrical store vanished; its front window
forever smeared by noses and hands of kids, agog
for the flickering wonder of black and white TV.
Next door, a noodle bar where I bought Beatles
and Rolling Stones records.
Cheap as Chips used to be hardware—
flying foxes whizzed cash from counter to office,
hurtled back with docket and change.

A row of shops with a café replaced the garage
where my first love worked.
A fish shop morphed from fruit and veg;
an open secret that the greengrocer's daughter
sold condoms on the sly from the milk-bar.
Haberdashery has disappeared, with its pair
of spinster sisters, each holding court at her own
ornate silver cash register—antiques all.

Shopping List

he sought:
a bed warmer
cook come housemaid
sweet-tempered trophy playmate
unquestioning obedience

she sought:
a lover-companion
protector-provider
appreciation
happy-ever-after

he offered:
a cave, cold and damp
devised crude tools
chased away predators
hunted small dinosaurs
skinned and boned their carcasses
collected and stored firewood
made a basic bench with seats
planted his seed, gave her sprogs
assumed he owned her
kept her in line

she warmed:
the cave to make a home
used skins for bedding
fashioned simple cloaks and moccasins
gathered grains and berries
kept the fire burning and prepared meals
served him as she suckled babies
shushed them while he ate and slept;
initially tolerated those chafing chains
till they almost choked her—
when she broke them up.

Dinner Dance

Scars still healing, newly separated singles
determine to enjoy the night,
smiles firmly fixed in place.
We exchange greetings, order meals,
a combo tunes organ to guitar.
An eager buzz travels through the group
as the singer checks the key for 'Bad Moon Rising'.
Toes tap, possible partners sussed.
More women than men, always,
but everyone gets their chance.

A new male, combat wounds still raw,
meal untouched, but not the drink,
his misery spews out.
'Can't see my kids,
came home and they'd gone'.
Some of the group make kind-hearted noises
but don't want to rouse their own demons.
With mixed feelings, move away.
In time he'll come to terms with life,
eventually smile again.

But not yet. Not yet.
Till then, we all make do
with the monthly dinner dance.

Through the Wall

I never met the tenant from the front unit,
nor knew her name, though over time
patterns were established—like the whiff
of warm toast through my kitchen vent
each morning at 7.00 on the dot.

Party sounds were easy,
laughter, loud music, clink of glasses.
Non-stop beeps from next door meant
she was away for the weekend,
forgetting to turn off her alarm, again.

After work on a weekday, always a clomp
of high-heeled boots on bare boards,
then a crash as something never identified
hit the flimsy wood-grain panel
between our two bedrooms.

I cursed the thinness of that plywood
when woken from deep sleep
by lively bed banging, along with groans
of carnal rapture due to my neighbour's
odd Friday or Saturday night lover.

I was relieved we never bumped
into one another once I realised
just what she would hear
from my side...

In the Interim

Between optimism and desperation
lonely people dress up, sip drinks,
chat in bars, at the meat market,
checking out the opposite sex,
hoping, always hoping.

Between love's free-fall and a fresh start
there must be time to lick wounds
to learn lessons, lest the primal urge
tempts us to ignore good sense, hit rocks
strewn along a road best not travelled.

Between waiting and mating
'hello' and 'how about it?' play their part.
Lonely hearts columns may be passé,
now it's eHarmony, Zoosk, Bumble
or Tinder—swipe right, check for likes.

Between mating and waiting
we wonder if things move too fast
or not fast enough. In a Network Society,
you may never get it right, no matter
how many times you go through it.

Safeguards

Stakeholders agreed
to build a stronghold
on rock-solid foundations,
faithful to the plan, immune to assault,
lasting all the ages—to pass on
with life's lessons learnt.
Teamwork ensured all worked well:
clear-cut routines became second nature,
kept defences strong.

Then stress turned light to dark—
they hardly noticed cracks
as mortar broke down
until their refuge teetered on the brink.
Those promises for upkeep
made in haste, lapsed too easily
without awareness.

Time to restart—
relationships are like that.

Once More

There are advantages
in being a born-again single—
no arguments at long phone calls
dishes can pile up, if they're used
no-one minds how late you stay out
or if you don't come home at all
no-one cares about those slap-dash meals
of cheese with Jatz and the spritz of Lambrusco
when that's all you can be bothered with
not a soul to hear a bathroom voice
singing along with Françoise Hardy
songs of loss and yearning.
Tell yourself you don't miss romance—
could write a book about the bad ones.

After many hits and misses
you meet someone who seems promising—
after the thrust and parry of newness
you dare to dream, trust, again.
When he cooks dinner, you relax, feet up
with a book plus a good red or two
relish the aroma of pasta
almost taste that peppery sauce
garlic with tomato, rich, lingering
while a haunting shakuhachi CD
quietly plays—and you can't quite recall
the benefits of being single.

A Most Unlikely Love Letter

For David

It was a child-like scrawl in pencil on the back
of a recycled scrap with printer ink blotches,
shoved into my letterbox.

I am cooking spaghetti for tea, it read,
with a vegetarian, tomatoey, garlicky sauce.
Nothing fancy.
If you want to join me, no need to call first,
just be at my joint by 6.40pm so I've got time
to put on enough pasta for both of us.

I walked past the four houses between us
to enjoy the meal with a couple of hearty reds,
content, all the more since I wasn't cooking.
Conversation—warm, disarming.

A weird start, promising more to come
with his suggestion down the track a-ways,
that in spite of our separate disasters,
it seemed right that we marry.

Backyard nuptials, vows exchanged
to Procol Harum's fantasy, he was unfazed
by bare feet, flowers in my long white hair
like a middle-aged hippy.

He's not the only one born with a quirky gene.

Glenda

We said farewell
soon after a sudden encounter.
Instant recognition surprised us both;
it's a long time since school.

We exchange news, a mere précis,
find what we had in common has gone.
She, with her tummy tuck,
frown-free face and bouncy breasts,
holiday unit at Surfers
and travel to Europe and the USA.

We make no promise to meet again.
I don't invite her to meet my man
but watch her waltz away along the beach,
tossing her shiny chestnut mane,
legs long and brown in that black bikini.

Alone.

Autumn Morning

On the beach, too cold to hold hands
our breath just smudges of ghostly mist
noses run in air crisp as rime
ears tingle like a secret pleasure.

Waves build and break
as surfers bob like cormorants
at their favourite reef break
a lone rider appears on a crest,
then drops.

In disgust, aloud, you urge the rest on,
know you could have caught those waves.
I wish you could be young enough again.
to join them.

But not so young
that on bitter autumn mornings,
like a surfing widow,
I'd be watching, always watching
from the beach.

By Her Own Hand

In Memory of Sonia

She left work early,
drove down a steep track
to a secluded spot
on the northern outskirts;
parked under gum trees.

Did you smell the sea air,
hear the tide lapping the shore
or notice the town lights
wink across the bay—
were you too hyped up to care?

She thought of loved ones,
those who made her world whole—
teenage children, parents,
friends, true to the end,
husband, her soul mate.

Would he understand?
Unwilling to leave but unable
to cope with his cancer's growth.
Too painful to watch him suffer,
or live without him.

Did you smell the sea air,
hear the tide lapping the shore
or notice the town lights
wink across the bay—
were you past the point of no return?

Ditching the Guff

Car doors locked, note written,
bourbon waiting.
Unscrewed the lid; liquor burned
as it washed down sleeping pills
prescribed by a misguided doctor.

Did you smell the sea air,
hear the tide lapping the shore
or notice the town lights
wink across the bay—
did you finally find peace?

Could Have Been My Story

Sounds of angry voices
hers—young, bitter
his—swearing, defiant
with cock-sparrow bravado.
Female pleading grows to banshee wail
a car door slams, tyres squeal
the *take that* attitude of a teen anthem.

Alone on the beach, she's hunched, forlorn
doesn't notice me skirt around—
I smother an urge to comfort.
This girl, the same age as my grandchild
could be embarrassed, prickly,
might she scorn sympathy?

I didn't have tattoos,
or piercings through lips and nose,
but some things are timeless.
I was seventeen once.

Grease Monkeys

In my home town fifty years ago,
boys became apprentices.
Grubby hands, grease-blackened overalls
set them apart, while a high-octane whiff
followed them, embedded in cotton scraps
stuffed into back pockets—
their badge of office.

They tinkered with their old jalopies,
treasures which inspired
dreams of a good life—
as their own boss.

Now, computerised cars with alien innards
spawn different credentials. Still,
the few are prepared to go the distance,
the siren-call strong.
Dirty hands a testament.

Legacy

When I open the saucepan cupboard,
stored cake racks give off the fragrance
of Golden Syrup, butter and coconut
embedded from umpteen batches
of Nutties, my mother's version of Anzacs.

I turn the pages of Mum's neat hand-written folder,
its separate sections for the tried and true.
There are recipes for Cinzano-laced fruit punch
and Pink Star Wine, her favourite boozy brews.
I find gems like Chocolate Self-saucing Pudding,
Yoghurt Devil's Food Cake as well as Nutties.

The wood stove was warm, welcoming—Mum wore
an apron over an old cotton dress, cheeks aglow,
using a tea-towel to remove hot trays from the oven.
Mouth-watering aromas filled the kitchen—
my fingers remember the smack
as I tried to taste before the biscuits cooled.

For years, memories of dead grandfathers
extended to the pungent earthiness of Dr Pat
seeping from pipe racks, still affixed to walls.
I'd die content if the perfume that was my memorial
was that motherly whiff of Golden Syrup,
butter and coconut, offering brief comfort,
the same way I recall my Mum.

A set of Wheels

We are born, only to become clapped-out.
On delivery, Mini Minors, no bells
or whistles till we pass through
the awkward chubby phase of V-Dubs.

In puberty, many a girl's body-work blushes
when brash young mechanics
ask for a hand to tighten their nuts.
or offer to check her grease nipples, free.

At maturity, we become the family sedan,
workhorse Kingswood or Falcon.
While some see themselves as a red-hot
Ferrari or Jag, most of us are built for comfort
more than speed.

Miles on the clock means rust patches
or valve bounce, burnt out mufflers
have a distinctly anal air.
The least you can expect is stiff joints
and if king-pins go, it's a hoist job for sure.

Further down the road, worn parts replaced
by almost good-as-new, a face-lift gives a boost:
skin-deep, since the chassis stays the same.
To no avail, we wind up, all,
on that Scrap Heap in the sky.

Yesterdays and Tomorrow

The person I was lives in me still,
not quite hidden behind fading flesh
and worrisome wrinkles.
Every moment adds further depth
to the shadow dogging my heels.

Who I may yet become
is a glow just around the corner
I can't quite grasp,
with a spring-time promise
like blossoms on fruit trees.

The apricot, peach and plum
shed confetti of pink and white petals,
yet still produce fruit
for us to savour
and discard the stone.

When the crop is spent,
we prune extraneous branches—
so the tree will be stronger
next year.

Sculpting Poems

If I wrote like Leonardo da Vinci
I'd compose sonnets to rival Shakespeare.
With rhymes inspired by the Bard,
my text would come alive in fourteen lines,
blaze across eons, while Gods of Talent
wept at their beauty.
Or perhaps not.

If I wrote like Henry Moore
I'd know all the rules and break them
with my larger-than-life free-form prose;
pure allegory to confound critics
as with chickens and red wheelbarrows.
That's not likely either.

If I wrote like Silvio Apponyi
I'd whittle words the way he carved a giant bilby.
Chips of chocolate flew from his chainsaw
as he toiled over 100kg of Melba's finest.
Consonants would pour from my pen,
create a seamless poetic voice
sweet enough for anyone.

Matriarch

Gone, the mainspring of our line
plus any family secrets not shared.
Her last battle lost, no more Gossip Central,
no conduit for news.

Nothing to do but distribute
a lifetime's possessions, though
in her usual organised way,
my mother labelled myriad items
with each recipient's name—
so that no one would argue.

There was poignancy on finding a 21st key
with a card from Dad and another
for their first anniversary. Also, well hidden,
a letter and book from a lover, spurned
when Father swept Mum off her feet.

We joked about Mum's fear of escalators,
hassles it caused in crowds and foreign cities
but can see the funny side now.
We swap stories of seeing her face reflected
in our mirrors—just glad her zest for life
and sense of humour were passed on as well.

Then a son-in-law's chance remark hits home;
as the eldest sibling, it's that moniker—
'Matriarch' now handed down to me.

Caffeine Fix

His morning ritual, complete,
coffee beans ground in the all-purpose mill,
measured, plunged,
an infusion rich as treacle.

My nose twitches; the mixture is exotic,
reminding me of an Egyptian souk;
a trader's dark eyes sparrow bright in his swarthy
face, the man pleads, 'Hey lady, you want spices?'
I sip. What has my husband done to this brew?
Though still the Espresso blend of old,
memories magnify; saffron, nutmeg, cinnamon,
arrayed in mounds of gold, red and brown.
Through pungent steam, my imagination runs riot.
I see shapely bodies seduce with belly-dance
and I'm positive I hear Darbuka drums and zills.

We finish our drink.
Baffled by his sphinx-like smile, I peer
into the grinder see the remnants
of this morning's grind,
smell the cumin from his last marinade,
mingled between the blades.

He reckons life is more exciting that way.

Still Learning

For Ebony

Seven-year-old wordsmith,
an imperious princess,
demands biscuits, drink.
Her mother prompts with,
'What's the magic word?'

This child reads a dictionary
with enthusiasm usually reserved
for adventure books.
Has a teenager's vocabulary.

Eyes raised, mouth open,
finger on bottom lip;
in a flash of insight,
my granddaughter proclaims,
'Abracadabra.'

Safe Bet

When they replaced the gutters
the salesman said
the job would be good for fifteen years.
You think that should just about see us out.
I'm not so sure—yes, by then you'll be ninety
but I'll just be a sprightly eighty-two.

Next, we ordered a rainwater tank
it sits on its stand, squat, green,
intending to catch every drop of rain.
Delivery man tells us
the tank's guaranteed for twenty-five years.
You look at me, we laugh, and I wonder.

Will you still want me to hold the ladder steady
make your knobbly knees knock
if I slither my fingers up the leg of your shorts
when you climb those steps to clear the gutters,
over twenty-five years, when you'll hit the ton
but I'll just be a sprightly ninety-two?

Number 24

The place I called home for over two years
lies empty—a house built arse-about;
a wall of lounge room windows looked out
on a Norfolk Island Pine and back fence.
Kitchen, bathroom, laundry peered
at a rickety Hills Hoist, a leafless metal tree
planted dead centre of the front lawn.

There's no china in the '50s retro cabinets.
A sunny enclosed porch that once held
my white wicker chairs and tiny table, bare.
Now, the built-in seating in the living room
hides traps for uninvited mousy guests.

After sharing a bedroom as a child
then married, still sharing; when I became
suddenly solo again, life was a mixed bag.
Lodging with friends, renting apartments
small and noisy, till number 24
became my haven.

It was hard to move,
even just six doors away
for a new life with a much-loved partner,
sharing again.
These days I can walk past,
no need to look in.

Adoption Adaption

It was a cautious settling in for me,
in this house my husband's grandfather built
ninety-five years ago, sweating in suit, hat, tie,
with a mob of men corralled like cattle
into a marquee on Moana beach,
for the first release of land.

That middle-aged gent measured, hammered,
covered frames with jarrah planks,
garnered what materials were around
with market in free fall.
It was not my family who trod these floors
over three generations,
leaving more than dusty footprints.

I've accepted this old lady's quirks—
her weatherboard kitchen walls,
endless grunge seeping through gaps,
rough, uneven cement floor, joists so sparse
that floorboards creak.

If my hubby's grandad visited, would he recognise
the cottage he built that once stood alone,
now the odd one amid tasteless concrete boxes?
Yes, we built in the verandahs for extra space,
replacing salt, sand and wind-weathered walls
but hope he'd know we've retained his home's
unique spirit, the calm of an oasis. I feel
it welcomed the changes with me, as I have gladly
adopted its aura of peace.

About the Author

Veronica was born in Port Lincoln, moving to Adelaide when personal circumstances made it necessary. She now sees herself as a story-teller, focusing on memories of her early years and the changes involved.

Some of the changes have been work related, from secretarial to factory to hospital seamstress, dry cleaning to support in schools. Once life in the city settled down, part time employment gave her long weekends free to travel around the countryside for over twenty years as a palmist in a group with other psychics, meeting the wild, the weird and the wonderful.

Veronica's work has been published in various magazines and collections here, interstate and New Zealand, as well as Friendly Street Anthologies since 2007. In 2019, she co-edited Friendly Street Anthology 43, (*alchemy*). In 2021 she was one of three selected by Friendly Street Poets' manuscript prize for novices, New Poets 22. In 2023 she co-edited Friendly Street Anthology 47, (*beyond the bend*).

Since 2011 she has been a member of Ochre Coast Poets, based south of Adelaide. This is her first full-length anthology. She lives in Moana with husband David and 'Wobbly', an untamed arthritic magpie.

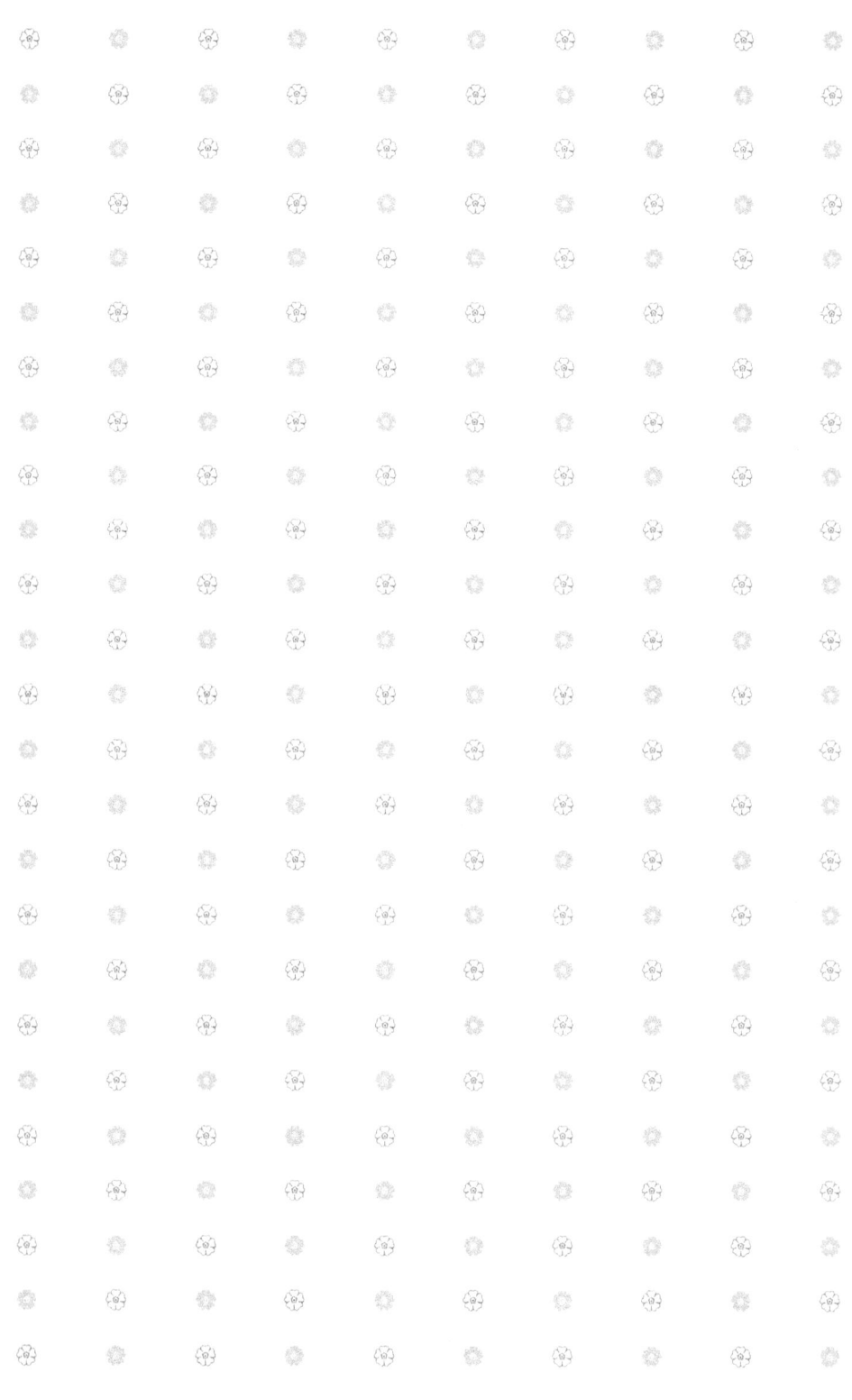

www.ingramcontent.com/pod-product-compliance
Lightning Source LLC
Chambersburg PA
CBHW060407080526
44583CB00012B/493